Beginning Rock Guitar

By Artie Traum.

Exclusive Distributors:
Music Sales Corporation
257 Park Avenue South, New York, NY 10010 USA
Music Sales Limited
8/9 Frith Street, London W1V 5TZ England
Music Sales Pty. Limited
120 Rothschild Street, Rosebery, Sydney, NSW 2018, Australia

Copyright © 1985 by Amsco Publications,
A Division of Music Sales Corporation, New York, NY.

Order No. AM 37292
US International Standard Book Number: 0.8256.2444.4
UK International Standard Book Number: 0.7119.0796.X

Book design by Nina Clayton
Cover design by Alison Fenton
Cover photography by Peter Wood
Interior photographs by Barbara Nitke
Modelled by Steve Tarshis
Edited by Amy Appleby and Peter Pickow

Printed in the United States of America by
Vicks Lithograph and Printing Corporation

Amsco Publications
New York/London/Sydney

CONTENTS

INTRODUCTION

Chuck Berry . . . Eric Clapton . . . Bo Diddley . . . Jimi Hendrix . . . Eddie Van Halen—the list of guitarists in rock and roll's hall of fame gets longer every year. New styles and innovations have continued to revolutionize rock guitar playing since its early days in the 1950s, when disc jockey Alan Freed first coined the phrase 'rock and roll'. Thousands—perhaps millions—of guitar fans have struggled on their electric guitars since then, shattering their neighbors' eardrums while trying to recreate the compelling sounds they have heard on record, in concert, or on television. Some players, like the incredibly creative Eddie Van Halen, seem to rise to the top of the heap with amazing speed. But most strum at home for their personal enjoyment, unravelling the mysteries of the guitar at their own pace.

When I was growing up in the 1960s, a sense of tradition tied rock guitarists to the blues of the past—particularly the urban blues from Chicago, Memphis, Detroit, and New Orleans. Players like B.B. King, Elmore James, and Albert King had a powerful influence on the rock players of the time. Indeed, most rock guitarists still rely on the blues scales, including string-bending, shuffle licks, and minor notes played against major chords. As writer Samuel Charters wrote in his fascinating book, *Country Blues:* "Rock and roll took the postwar blues singing style and set it against a rhythm with repetitive chords on piano or guitar . . . the effect was overpowering."

Of course, things have come a long way since then. But as New Orleans blues/jazz/pop guitarist Clarence "Gatemouth" Brown says, "All American popular music derives from the blues. You simply can't play rock and roll or jazz, unless you have a solid blues foundation. . . ." Indeed, all rock guitarists worth their salt—from Eric Clapton to Jimmy Page, from Carlos Santana to Bonnie Raitt, from Jeff Beck to Nancy Wilson—have noted their debt to the blues. Many rock guitarists began by playing backup to singers. People like Scotty Moore and James Burton found themselves tossing in licks and riffs to embellish the vocals of performers like Elvis Presley, Rick Nelson, and Buddy Holly. These musicians learned their twelve-bar blues styles first, as well as various country-music styles, before branching out into uncharted territory. Just as an abstract painter must study the classics before expressing his or her art, I strongly recommend that you study the roots of rock first.

"I got an early introduction to rhythm and blues music when I was just sixteen," Pete Townshend of The Who once said. "I was into stuff like John Lee Hooker, Jimmy Reed, and B.B. King before anyone else. . . ." Many rock players, including the Rolling Stones, Clapton, and Hendrix, were under the spell of urban blues for years before breaking out into their own dynamic styles. We will begin our study of rock and roll guitar in the same manner—with the blues, a touch of country music, and some basic chords.

The guitar is an incredibly versatile instrument and the sounds, effects, and melodies that emerge from it constantly amaze me. Still, one has to start at the beginning. Where else? Jimmy Page, leader of Led Zeppelin, said he "started out very slowly" with an old steel-stringed Spanish guitar that his parents had in the house. "I went to guitar shops, watching what people were doing, trying to learn. In the end, it was the other way, and people were watching me." Page, however, had no patience for guitar lessons. He made his own way on the instrument by "spending hours trying to figure out" the riffs and chords on the records he loved. "The first ones were Buddy Holly chord solos," he told John Tobler and Stuart Grundy in an interview from their book *The Guitar Greats*," . . . songs like 'Peggy Sue.' The next step was definitely James Burton [the lead guitarist on Ricky Nelson's records]. It was the bending string style that really got me going."

Many guitarists have learned their craft by watching the people they respect and admire, listening closely to their records and tapes, and taking lessons. Of course, instruction books can give you many helpful hints and point you in the right direction. Books can show you notes, chords, and strumming ideas, but it's up to you to put grace and feeling into your playing. As Ry Cooder once said: "You have to learn where it's coming from . . . that's the important part."

I would suggest that you invest in, or borrow, records that show different rock guitar styles and study them closely. Get front-row seats at concerts to watch the lead and rhythm guitarists' hands. Get together with friends and exchange licks and riffs. Try audio instruction tapes. Homespun Tapes, for example, puts out useful instruction tapes on many different styles. Most important, however, is to stick with it. Don't give up. Guitar playing, particularly good rock and roll, takes long hours of practice and dedication. Still, it should be fun for you!

Just after completing his *Electric Ladyland* album, Jimi Hendrix told an interviewer, "If you can do your own thing—do it properly. You have to set some heavy goals to keep yourself going." Hendrix certainly passed this advice on to the younger generation of players. "Hendrix did things that nobody else has been able to do," Eddie Van Halen said recently. "I used to listen to his records and try to pick up ideas."

Listening . . . studying . . . watching and *trying:* that's all to ask of yourself when undertaking any new study.

"You've got to practice for years to be able to do the things I do," Eddie Van Halen said. That is certainly true! Yet one need not be an Eddie Van Halen to enjoy the guitar. Some of us are destined to enjoy jamming with friends at parties, or just fooling around in the living room at home. Wherever your destiny may lead you, you must start where thousands of musicians before you started—with basic chords, riffs, strums, and songs. That's the fun right there. "I'd have been locked up long ago if I hadn't had a guitar," Jeff Beck once said. Indeed, Jeff Beck speaks for a lot of us!

A Word on Equipment

Rock guitarists love equipment. They are always adding tremolo bars, effects pedals, and other gadgets to their collections. Right now, you won't need any of that. The material in this book, in fact, could be played on a simple acoustic guitar—although an electric guitar plugged into a small amplifier is probably the best setup. In general, electric guitars are easier to play than acoustics. Bending strings, for example, is much easier to do on an electric since the strings are lighter and more flexible. But, at this point, it's not absolutely necessary to go electric.

Whatever guitar you choose, there are a few pointers that will make your playing more fun. First of all, your instrument should have a straight neck, easy action, and tone controls that give you the sound you want. Later on, you will have to decide if you want to have a funky, bluesy sound like B.B. King, Jimmy Page, or Bonnie Raitt—or a smoother, slicker sound like John Hall or George Benson. Extensive tone controls can create almost all of these sounds. A *solid-body* guitar will give more bite to your sound, while *hollow-body* guitars will sound somewhat mellow. Hollow-body guitars were originally acoustic guitars with electric pickups mounted in them to produce a jazzy, rounded tone. Since they feed back more easily at high volume levels, they can cause problems if you wish to play very loudly.

Classic rock guitars, like the Fender Stratocaster, Telecaster, Broadcaster, or the Gibson Les Paul, are in great demand these days. At this point, don't let your ego decide which guitar to buy. Sure, it's nice to have the very best guitar around, but many companies make instruments at reasonable prices. Look into Washburn, Guild, or some of the Japanese imports. There are terrific bargains available on the market today.

Amplifiers

The selection of an amp is largely a matter of your personal preference. Guitarists seem to trade them in every few months to experiment with something new. When Jimi Hendrix first came to New York, he used a Les Paul guitar played through a small Fender amp. At that time, he was playing in a small club in Greenwich Village. By the time his first record climbed the charts, he was playing a Fender Stratocaster through a 200-watt Marshall amp—with all the controls set at the maximum limit!

By contrast, guitarists like J.J. Cale, Amos Garrett, and Bonnie Raitt play through simple, unadorned setups. For your purposes, simply make sure that you can get a clear, crisp sound from your amplifier. Later on, you'll want to experiment with the volume controls. For now, keep it simple.

Holding the Guitar

Come on, you say, anyone can hold a guitar. That's true. But it is important to be comfortable while you are making your first attempt at chords and scales. Find a straight-backed chair (without arms) to sit in, and hold the guitar on your lap. Once you are seated comfortably, you will be looking down at the guitar from a bird's-eye view. Off to your left, at the end, you will find the *peghead* with the *tuning pegs* attached. Attached to the tuning pegs are *strings*, which run all the way along the *neck* to the *bridge* of the guitar. You will have to reach over and adjust the tuning pegs to tune your guitar. You must learn to tune properly. It will take some time, but after a while it will become second nature to you.

Tuning

Look down at the strings. The string closest to you is called the low E-string. It is the thickest string. Guitarists usually start tuning with this string— although you may want to start with another string once you are familiar with the tuning process.

As you can see from the diagram below, there are six strings on your instrument. The are named as follows:

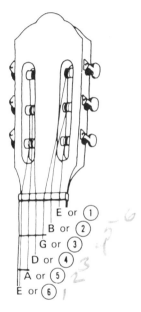

E or (1)
B or (2)
G or (3)
D or (4)
A or (5)
E or (6)

There are several ways to approach the tuning proc-ess. The easiest is to use an electronic tuner. These devices can make tuning very simple and will help you develop your ear at the same time. They are not terribly expensive and I strongly recommend invest-ing in one. You'll never be out of tune again. You will also get immediate visual feedback from your tuner to show whether a string is sharp or flat. You simply dial the note you want and then tune the strings to it.

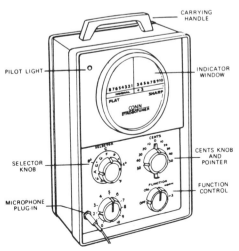

Amateur rock guitarists often have a problem keeping their instruments in tune. Rock playing makes more physical demands on the instrument than folk or classical guitar playing. Every time you bend a string or strum through a series of funky rhythm parts, your guitar is likely to lose its tuning. So rock guitarists must check their tuning often to make sure the strings are still true. An out-of-tune guitar can throw an entire band into chaos. As Livingston Taylor says: "A guitarist must be perfectly in tune. There is no reason in this day and age to be out of tune. . . ."

If you do not have an electronic tuner, you can use a tuning fork to obtain a true A note—which corresponds to the open fifth string of the guitar. Then you can tune the other strings to that. For example, if you fret (press) the E string (sixth string) at the 5th fret, it should equal an A note (the open fifth string). Likewise, the A string (fifth string) fretted at the 5th fret will give you a D note (the open fourth string). The D string (fourth string) fretted at the 5th fret should equal a G note (the open third string). The G string (third string) fretted at the 4th fret will give you a B note (the open second string) and the B string (second string) fretted at the 5th fret will give you an E note (the open first string). Many guitarists use this method to adjust their strings when they suspect a string has gone flat or sharp.

CHORDS: THE FOUNDATION OF ROCK AND ROLL

Everybody wants to be a lead guitarist these days, jumping into the spotlight by playing a series of notes that soar into the stratosphere. Yet, the rhythm guitarist is perhaps the most interesting player in a band. Rhythm-guitar parts must link the drummer to the bass player, and provide a foundation for the lead vocalist or the lead instrumentalist to sing or play over. Some rhythm players, like Steve Cropper and Curtis Mayfield, have become legendary for their unique ability to find a *groove*. Indeed, a strong rhythm guitarist is a tremendous asset in any group.

The first thing you must learn in playing rhythm guitar is how to play the chords. And there are plenty of them. In fact, entire books have been filled with the thousands of chords that are possible on the guitar.

Well, let's get down to it. Let's start by looking at a chord diagram. A chord diagram is actually a head-on view of the fingerboard.

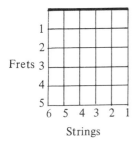

As you can see, each string has been assigned a number. The frets are also numbered, beginning with the fret closest to the nut. (The nut is represented by the thick line on top).

Of course, you will be using your left hand to play notes and chords, so we will need numbers for your fingers as well.

Let's start with an E chord—one that you'll use time and again in rock and roll. It looks like this:

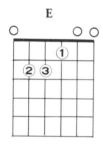

Make sure you do this correctly. Your first finger presses the third string at the 1st fret. Your second finger presses the fifth string at the 2nd fret. And your third finger presses the fourth string at the 2nd fret. You must push down with enough strength to make the notes sound clear, taking care that your other fingers don't block the open strings. In other words, arch your hands around the neck so that the sound comes out clearly. Strum down across the strings with your right hand and you should hear an E chord.

You'll notice that your fingers will start to become sore as you play these first chords. Don't worry about it; the more they hurt, the better you are doing. As they say in Olympic training: no pain, no gain. The soreness is only temporary; it *will* go away. After a while, you will develop callouses that will protect your fingers when playing.

Okay, let's get back to chords. Do you understand the E chord? Now, let's go on to the A chord. It looks like this:

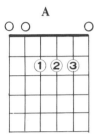

Line your fingers up for the chord. Now strum across all of the strings with your right hand. For now, curl the fingers of your right hand slightly as you strum. Later on, we'll get into using a pick.

If you are having trouble with the chords, press your thumb gently onto the back of the guitar neck as in this photograph. This will add the extra leverage you need.

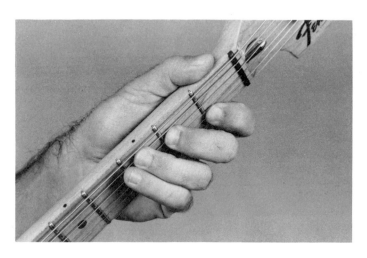

Make sure that your fingers are pressing the strings very close to the fret, without actually being on the fret itself. You don't have to strain to push down, but make sure you are exerting enough pressure so that the notes ring clearly. Keep the nails on your left hand rather short so they won't dig into the fingerboard. Your right-hand nails may stay long if you wish—particularly if you intend to play finger-style guitar at some point.

Now try going back and forth from the E chord to the A chord (slowly at first) with four beats to each chord:

The secret of playing guitar well is your ability to change chords at will. Each slash in the example above gets one strum with your right hand. As you change chords, check out how smooth your strumming is. It should be easy and effortless.

Let's try one more chord, the B7. When you have learned this one additional chord, you will have all the chords you need to play hundreds of bluesy songs in the key of E.

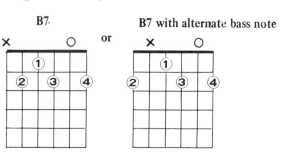

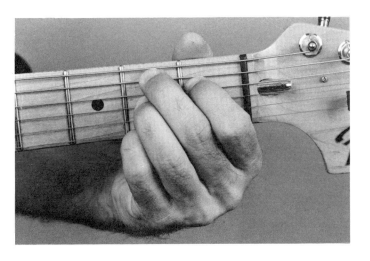

There is one more point I must mention. When you play the B7 chord, stay away from the low E-string while strumming. It will sound dissonant, or harsh to the ear, because it is not part of the chord. An alternate way to play B7 would be to move your second finger from the fifth to the sixth string. The second finger will *damp* the fifth string (stop it from sounding) and then you can strum *all* of the strings.

Here's a twelve-bar blues in E.

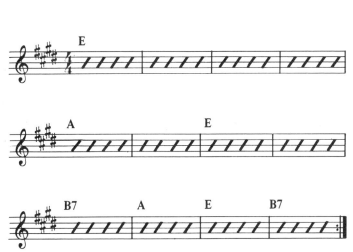

Good Mornin' Blues

We are getting into some relatively new territory here, but I'd like to get you playing as early as possible. Keep practicing these chord changes until you can play them easily. Once you can, you'll be able to play the first song, a popular blues called "Good Mornin' Blues."

Good Mornin' Blues

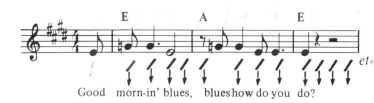

Good morn-in' blues, blues how do you do?

Good morn-in' blues, blues how do you

do? Well I'm do-in' all right,_ good

morn-in' how are you?

There are literally hundreds of blues songs that can be played with these chords. Once you have mastered the chords, you can try out other songs on your own. In the Bibliography, you will find a list of songbooks for further study.

Guitarist Pat Alger advises students to use an "economy of motion" when changing chords. Pat says, "Move your hands as little as possible," when he teaches students at guitar workshops. "Don't overshoot your mark." This is excellent advice; keep it in the back of your mind as you practice.

A Word About Practicing

"Practicing the guitar is like eating,"Carlos Santana said once in an interview. "If you don't discriminate what you eat, you get sick-indigestion. You digest music by learning it; it is stored in your memory cells." Carlos Santana's advice should be remembered as you study the guitar. After all, there is so much to learn, so much to absorb, and so much to

consider in music that it is important to be dis-
criminating. You should pick and choose what's important to you, and studiously go about learning it.
After a while, it will become a part of your memory
and you'll be able to play without even thinking
about it.

As a beginner, however, you will be faced with the
'frustration factor'. Practicing the guitar should be
fun, and usually it is. At times, however, you may
want to pick up your guitar and smash it into your
amplifier. Perhaps that's why Pete Townshend of
the Who smashed guitars during concerts in the
1970s.

My philosophy of practicing attempts to prevent
that degree of frustration. When a riff, chord, or
song stays just outside of your grasp . . . let it go
for a while. Simply forget it. After some time, come
back to it. It's funny sometimes how some things
click for musicians. Just when you think you'll never
get the knack of something, it suddenly becomes
clear—and easy!

Seventh Chords

The E7 and A7 chords will add some spice to your
playing as you learn the blues progression. They
look like this, and can be used in place of regular E
or A chords:

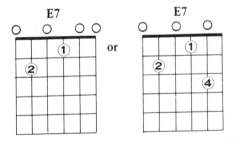

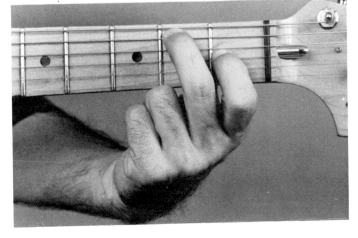

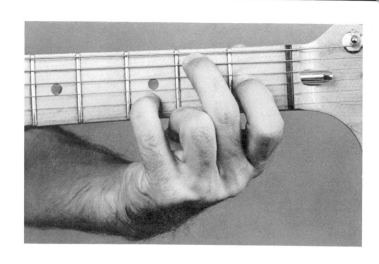

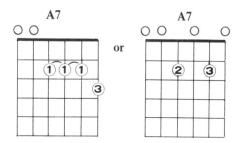

A7 or A7

Let's try the twelve-bar blues progression with the E7, A7, and B7 chords added.

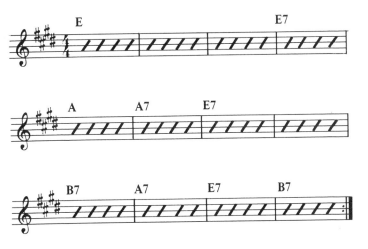

Now, let's try another blues song, using 7th chords instead of regular chords. Do you hear how the musical texture changes?

See See Rider

Chord Study

Here is a series of chords that you must learn in order to play rock and roll. Take your time and learn each key separately.

Key of A

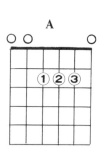

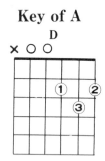

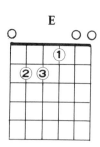

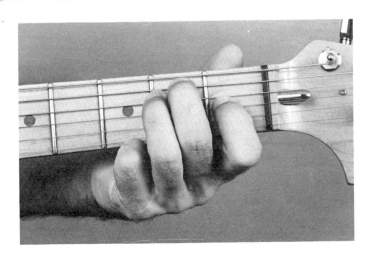

As you can see, some chords overlap between keys. In the key of A, both the A and E chords appear— yet they are used in a different context than they were in the key of E. Now, you can also play "Good Mornin' Blues" in the key of A. Transposed to A it would look and sound like this:

Good Mornin' Blues

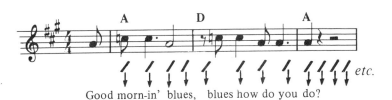

Good morn-in' blues, blues how do you do?

Good morn-in' blues, blues how do you

do? Well, I'm do-in' all right,_ good

morn-in', how are you?

Let's use some other new chords to play the same progression in different keys.

Key of D

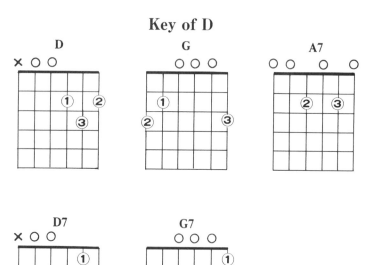

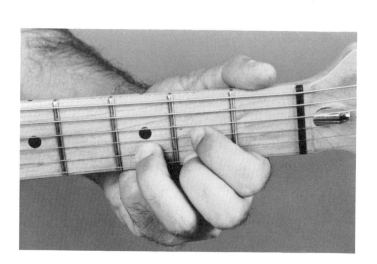

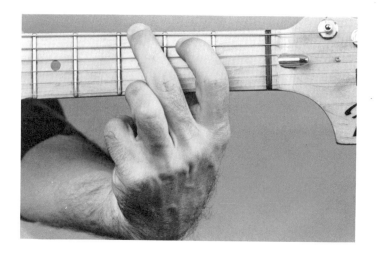

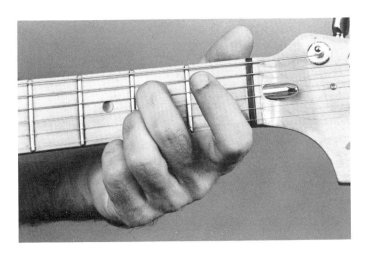

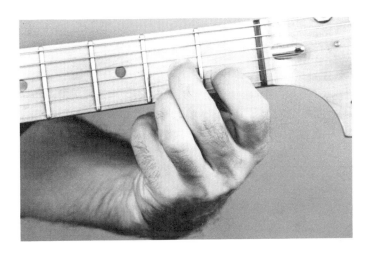

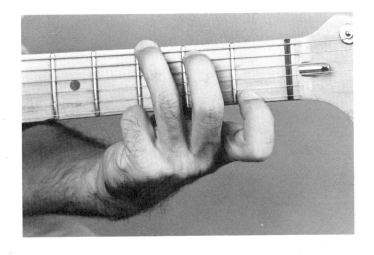

Twelve-Bar Blues Progression in the Key of D

Key of G

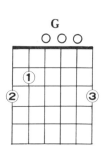

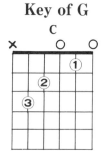

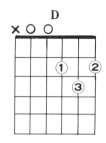

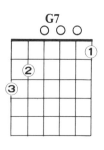

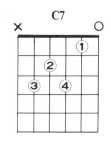

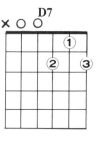

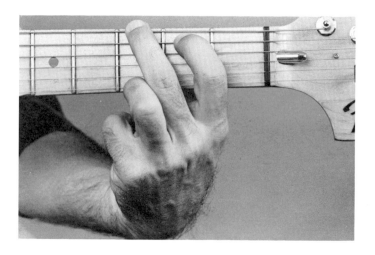

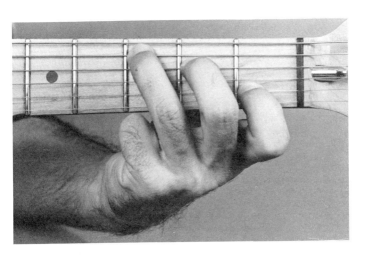

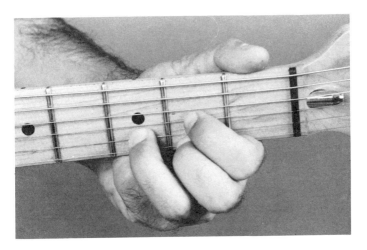

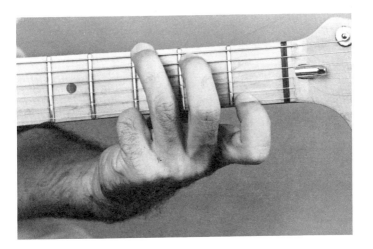

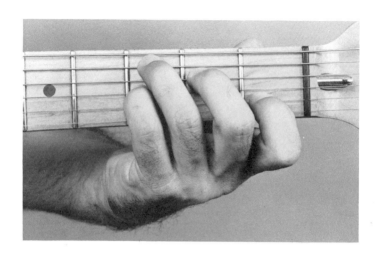

Twelve-Bar Blues Progression in the Key of G

Key of C

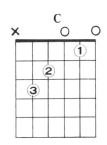

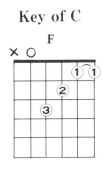

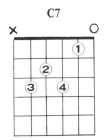

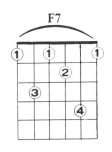

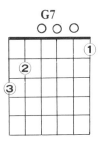

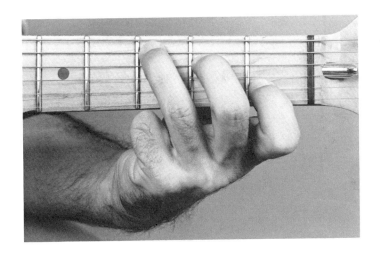

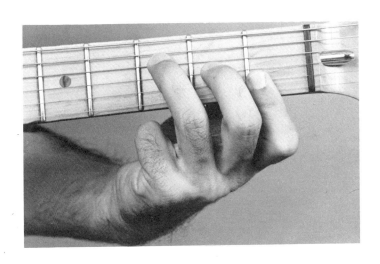

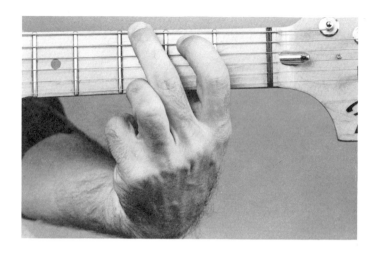

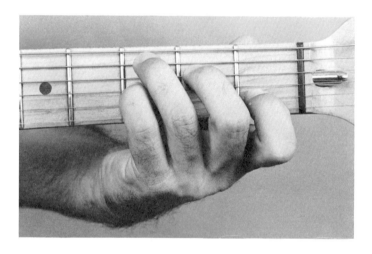

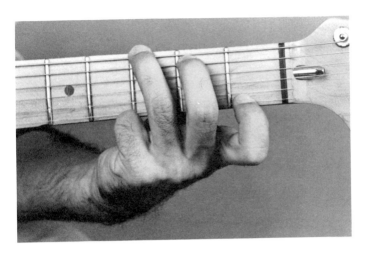

Twelve-Bar Blues Progression in the Key of C

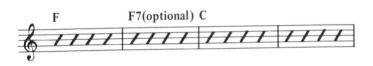

Reading Guitar Tablature and Music

Nancy Wilson, the lead guitarist of Heart, once said: "I think it's good to read music—but not necessarily for everybody. Ear training is really more important. I learned guitar mostly by ear. . . ." The debate over reading music for rock guitar will probably go on forever. The great, early players—Chuck Berry, Bo Diddley, Buddy Holly, and even Jimi Hendrix—did not read music at all. They learned entirely by ear. Later on, musicians began studying the elements of music carefully—the results were stunning! Just listen to George Benson solo sometime—the man knows his music theory.

Many guitarists use a system called 'tablature'. In tablature, there are six horizontal lines which represent the six strings of the guitar. The high E is on top. The other strings line up in order. Numbers placed on the lines indicate frets. I have notated the examples in the following section on the shuffle lick in tablature, as well as in standard notation.

Tablature will be of great value to you as you learn single-string riffs.

THE SHUFFLE LICK IN BLUES AND ROCK

In the early days of blues, guitarist like Robert Johnson, Bukka White, and Skip James accompanied their songs with a steady, thumping bass-riff known as "the shuffle lick." In those days, many guitarists didn't work with drummers or bass players, so they needed a bass-line moving with them. These and Buddy Holly—and eventually became a major factor in early rock and roll guitar playing. You can hear examples of this style on songs like Chuck Berry's "Memphis, Tennessee," "Johnny B. Goode," as well as many early Beatles songs. Indeed, the shuffle lick travelled to England in the early 1960s, returning to the U.S.A. with the Rolling Stones, the Dave Clark Five, the Yardbirds, and the Kinks—all of whom used the lick extensively. It is still used today, and will probably be with us for a long time to come. This riff is very simple to play, although playing it well is another matter.

The first example of the shuffle lick will be in the key of A, where it is easy to move from chord to chord. Essentially, you work with your fourth and fifth strings on an A chord. There are several things to keep in mind before you start to play. First, remember that you are going to play only two notes at a time. All other notes are *damped;* that is, either muffled with the fingers of the left or right hand, or simply avoided. The '×' at the top of the chord diagrams shows which notes to stay away from.

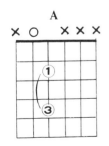
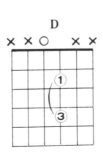
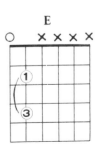

Let's start with the A chord. With your right hand pluck the fifth and fourth strings using your thumb and first finger—while fretting the fourth string at the 2nd fret with the first finger of the left hand. Then, move to the fourth string, 4th fret with the third finger (left hand) while plucking the strings again. Do this rhythmically, hitting each note *twice*, as shown below:

To do this with a D chord, simply move everything up to the fourth and third strings:

For an E chord, move everything down to the sixth and fifth strings:

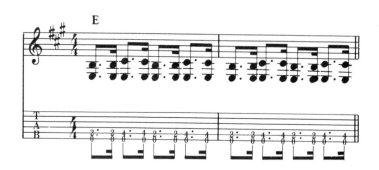

Now, let's try the shuffle lick all the way through a
twelve-bar blues in the key of A.

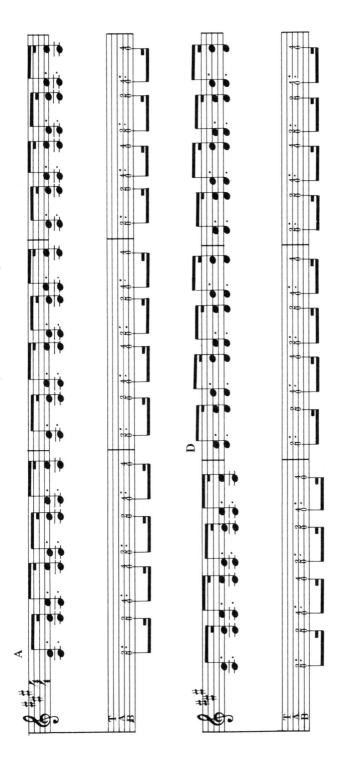

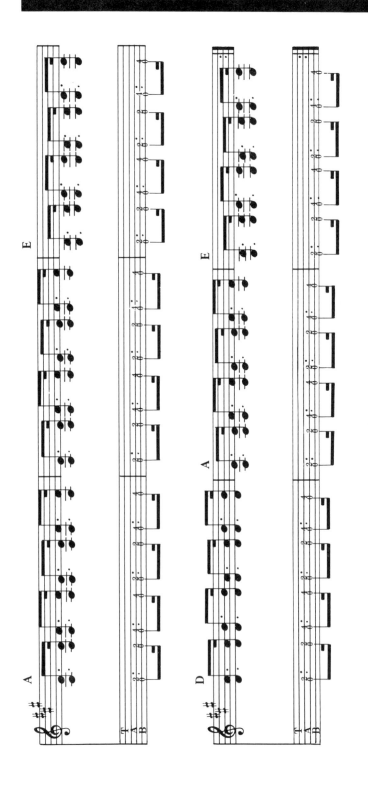

Using a Flatpick

Up to this point, we have been strumming and plucking with our fingers. Most rock guitarists, however, use a flatpick—although some prefer to use their fingers, or fingerpicks. Flatpicks come in three gauges—soft, medium, and hard. I'd suggest that you get a few different picks and experiment with them. The flatpick will feel bulky, awkward, and unruly at first—but after a while, you will get used to it. It will eventually become an extension of your right hand.

Flatpicks are generally made of plastic, although recently several small companies have started producing them from light metals. In the old days, guitarists loved the resilience of natural tortoise-shell picks. These turtles are now an endangered species, so don't go looking for tortoise-shell picks these days! I started playing with a soft pick becuase I found it easy to work with while learning how to play. Now I like the tough quality of a hard pick— which produces a bright, rounded tone. It is simply a matter of personal choice.

Hold the pick between your right thumb and index finger: not too tight, but not too loose either. As in most aspects of guitar playing, you need to exert a fair amount of pressure without overdoing it. Keep this in mind as you strum or hit single notes with the pick. The most distinctive quality of any good guitarist is his or her touch. I could care less that someone can play 3,000 notes per second. If you can play one note well—with grace, dignity, and feeling—then you are an ace musician in my book!

Midnight Special

"Midnight Special" is one of the most popular blues songs of all time, and it adapts perfectly to the shuffle lick. Keep in mind that the song begins on the D chord—even though it is in the key of A.

Midnight Special

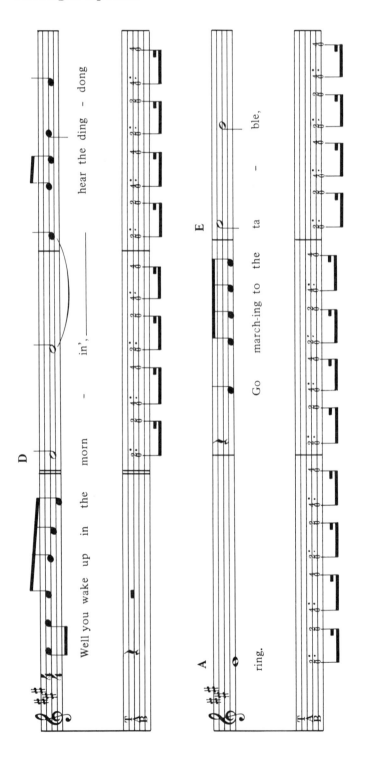

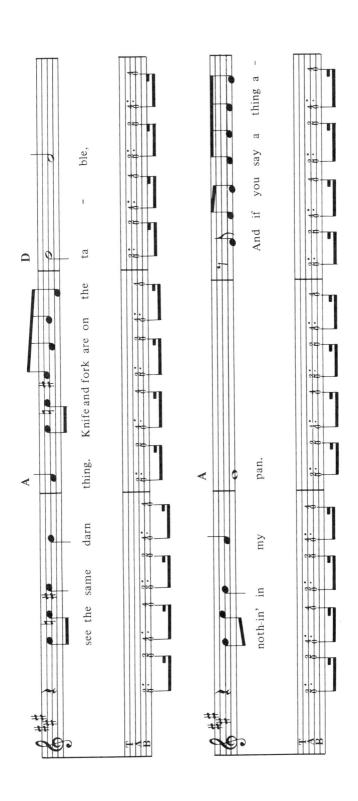

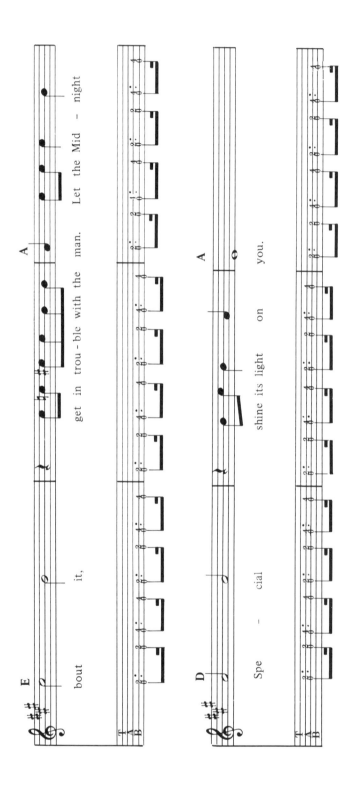

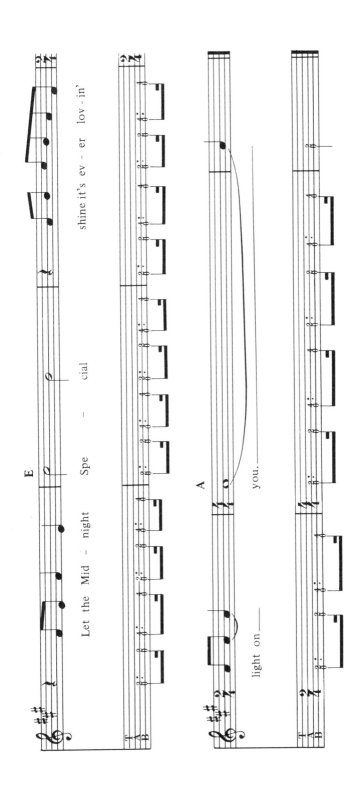

Shuffle Lick Variation

By adding one more note to the shuffle lick, we can obtain a much more interesting sound.

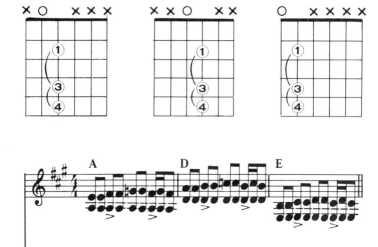

Listen to Chuck Berry's recording of "Memphis, Tennessee" to see how one of rock's greatest guitarists used this variation.

AN INTRODUCTION TO LEAD GUITAR

Okay, admit it—you really want to play lead guitar.
You want to leap around the stage with your hands
flailing across the fingerboard at breakneck speed!
Well, it's going to take some time and work. This
book will give you some pointers—and get you
started in the right direction.

Pentatonic Blues Scales

First of all, most rock and roll is based on the
pentatonic blues scale, which looks like this in the
key of E:

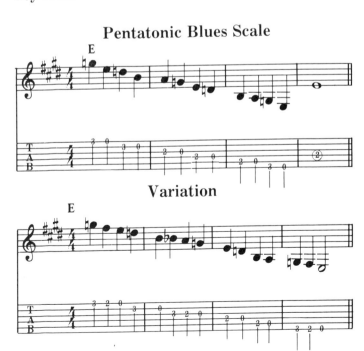

Pentatonic Blues Scale

Variation

Play these notes using your pick. For now, just use downward strokes (⊓). Later on, you'll want to go down (⊓) and up (∨) to increase your speed. These bluesy notes are amazingly versatile. For example, if you are in the key of E, these notes (for the most part) will sound fine with the A and B7 chords as well. So, you can play through an entire blues in E using just a few notes!

As you progress, you'll learn to move these notes up the neck and into different keys. Stick with these examples until you can find the notes easily. Mastering the jump from the first string all the way down to the sixth string will take some serious practice. When you are familiar with the notes, try starting on the third string, or the fifth string, and create a little blues melody of your own. There are a lot of possibilities available to you using just a few notes!

String Bending

Most teachers won't even mention string bending until the student has made considerable progress with his or her playing. But I think you should be familiar with it from the very start. In the early days of country-blues guitar—from 1910 to 1945— many players used a *bottleneck* or a hollow piece of metal to get a sliding, shiny sound from their guitars. This technique is still used today. It is the trademark of such players as Bonnie Raitt, Johnny Winter, Ry Cooder, and Taj Mahal. As the blues moved north after World War II, blues players like B.B. King and Albert King figured out a way to get the slide sound just by bending strings with their fingers. Today, string bending is an essential part of rock guitar playing and the mainstay of every good rock guitarist—from Clapton to Van Halen.

Light strings make string bending easier, but it is still a difficult technique. Generally, strings are bent upward—raising the pitch. Let's try one bend on the third string. Place the third finger of your left hand at the 7th fret of the third string. I know: it's hard! Hit the third string with your pick. As the string rings out, push it upward with your left hand. That's bending the string.

Now, there are many ways to bend a string and it may be years before you can do it properly. Still, keep this technique in mind as you continue your study of rock guitar. You might like to try it with the blues scale you have just learned. Pick the first string at the 3rd fret, and then push it upward as the string rings out. This should bend the string to a slightly higher pitch. Any note can be bent in rock playing and eventually you will find the proper places to make this exciting technique work for you!

Well, thanks for joining me in this overview of beginning rock guitar. I have tried to cover the basics and I hope you've enjoyed the journey with me. The Bibliography will help you find books that I think will take you much further in your studies. Keep playing. Don't give up. You'll find hours, days, months, and years of enjoyment with that guitar of yours!

CHORD
GLOSSARY

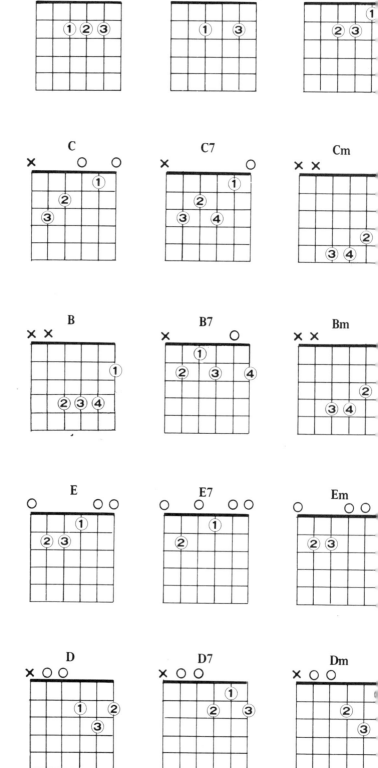

BIBLIOGRAPHY

Funaro, Arti and Traum, Artie. *Improvising Rock Guitar.* Oak Publications.

Guralnick, Peter. *Feel Like Going Home.* Random House.

Roth, Arlen. *Slide Guitar.* Oak Publications.

Shipton, Russ. *Rock 'n' Roll Chord Book.* Wise Publications.

Traum, Artie and Funaro, Arti. *Chicago Blues Guitar.* Oak Publications.